J599.2
BEN

CRANFORD LIBRARY

KANGAROOS AND OTHER MARSUPIALS

Design
David West
Children's Book Design
Illustrations
George Thompson
Picture Research
Cecilia Weston-Baker
Editor
Denny Robson
Consultant
John Stidworthy

© Aladdin Books Ltd

Designed and produced by
Aladdin Books Ltd
70 Old Compton Street
London W1

*First published in
Great Britain in 1988 by*
Franklin Watts
12a Golden Square
London W1

ISBN 0 86313 765 2

Printed in Belgium

This book tells you all about kangaroos and other pouched mammals – where they live, what they eat and how they survive. Find out some surprising facts in the boxes on each page. The identification chart will help you when you see kangaroos and their relatives in zoos, wildlife parks or in the wild.

The little square shows you the size of the animal. Each side represents 2m (6½ft.)

A red square means that the animal is in need of protection. See the survival file.

The picture opposite shows a possum sitting on a tree trunk

FIRST SIGHT

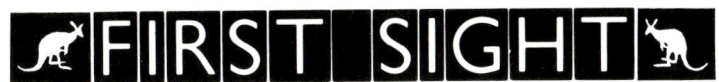

KANGAROOS AND OTHER MARSUPIALS

Lionel Bender

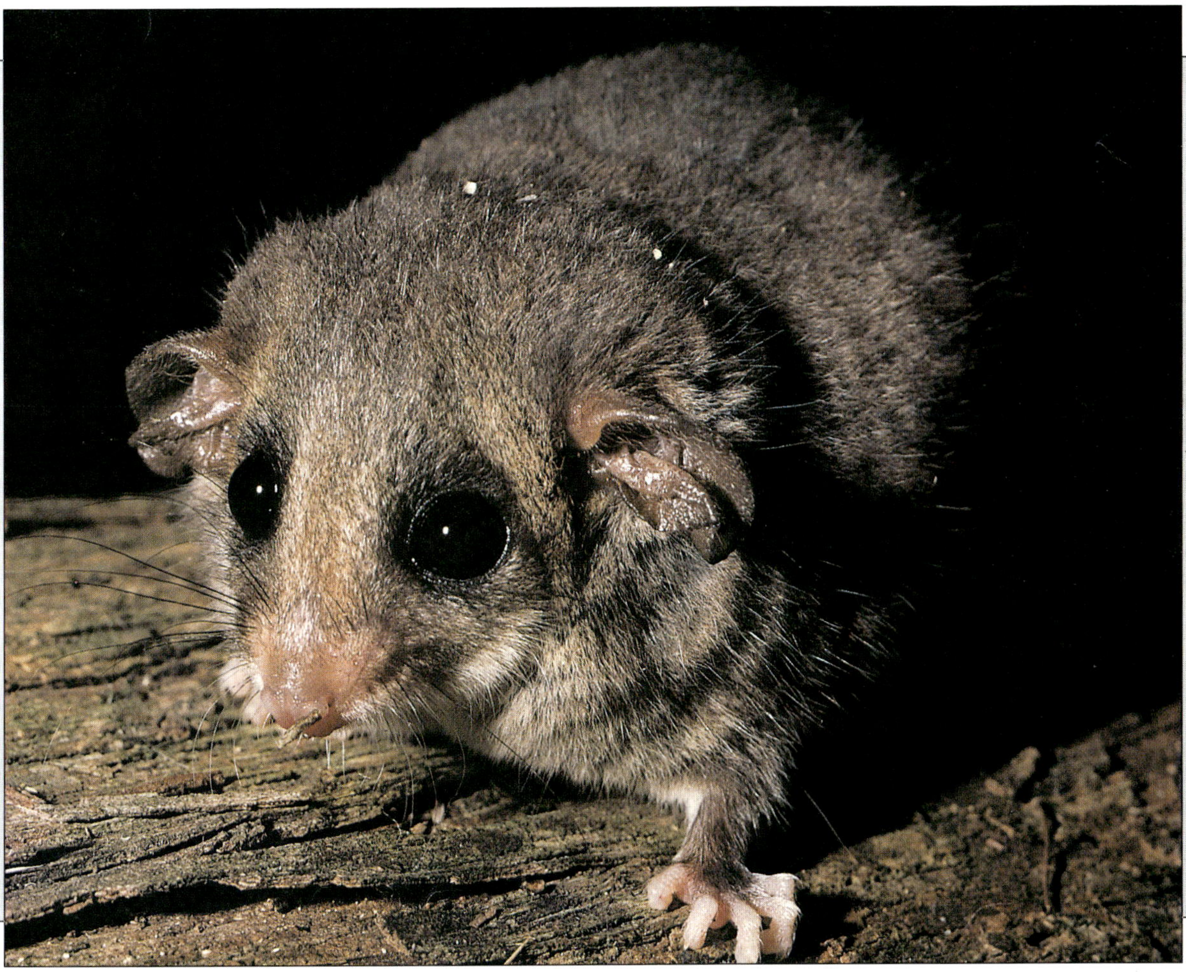

GLOUCESTER PRESS

London · New York · Toronto · Sydney

Introduction

Kangaroos are mammals, as we are. But unlike us, the newborn look nothing like their parents. After they are born they grow in a pouch outside their mother's belly. Pouched mammals are known as marsupials.

The kangaroo family includes three species of true kangaroo and 47 similar, smaller species known as wallabies. All members of the kangaroo family live in Australia and the islands nearby. They feed on grass and other plants, and inhabit grasslands and forests. In the same part of the world there are about 120 other species of marsupials. These include the Koala, wombats and the possums. There are also pouched mammals living in America. They are called opossums. There are about 80 species of opossum.

Contents
Pouched animals **7**
Hopping along **8**
Climbers, gliders and burrowers **11**
Plant-eaters **12**
Meat-eaters **14**
Daily life **17**
Social life **18**
Attack and defence **21**
Senses and scents **22**
Courtship and breeding **24**
Growing up **26**
Survival file **28**
Identification chart **30**
Make the Marsupial Game **30**
Index **32**

◁ **The Red Kangaroo is the largest marsupial**

Pouched animals

The largest pouched mammal, the Red Kangaroo, grows to 2m (6½ft) long and 90kg (200lb) in weight. But at birth, it is only 2cm (¾in) long and weighs about 1g (1/30 oz). The baby is born after developing inside its mother's womb for only five weeks. It spends the next six months inside her pouch feeding on milk.

The babies of most mammals grow and develop inside their mother's body until they are fully formed. They get all their food from a special structure inside the womb called a placenta. But female marsupials do not have placentas. Their babies must come out of the womb when very small and suckle milk constantly until they can look after themselves.

Pouched mammals have lifestyles like those of placental mammals. Kangaroos, for example, feed and behave like the antelope of Africa. There are pouched mammals that look exactly like placental mammals, such as wolves, cats and house mice.

marsupial mouse

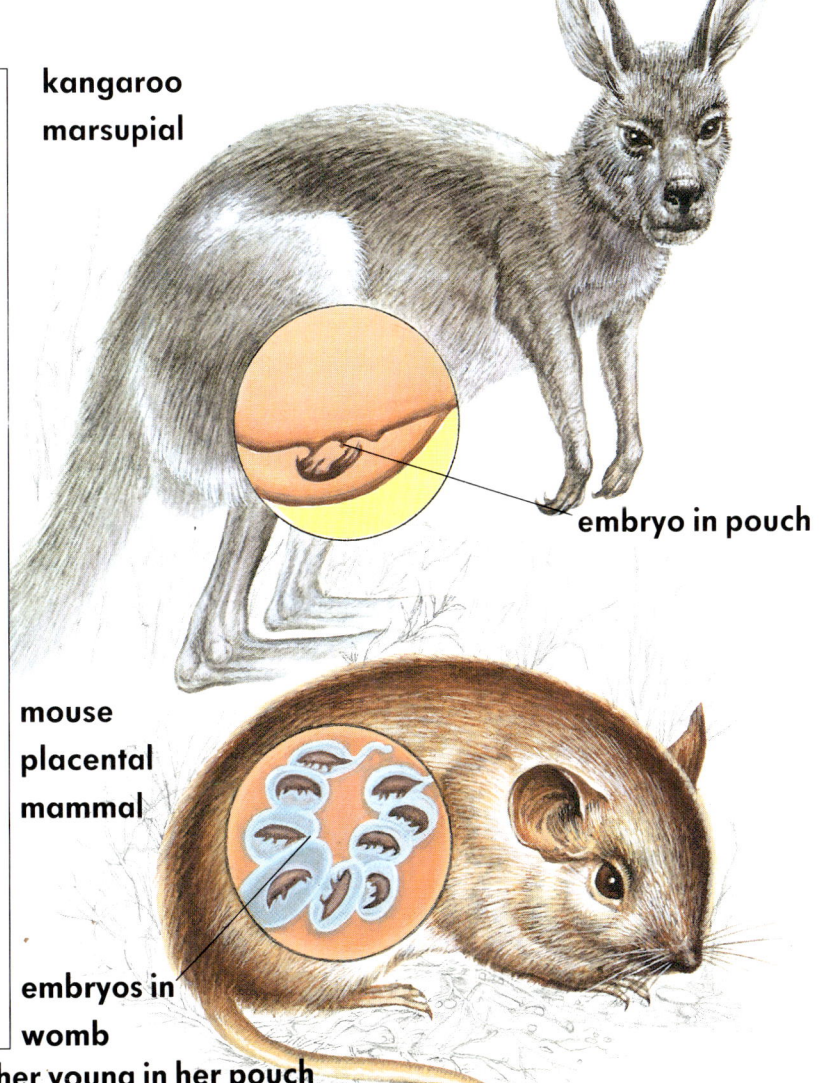
kangaroo marsupial
embryo in pouch
mouse placental mammal
embryos in womb

◁ A mother Grey Kangaroo with her young in her pouch

Hopping along

Kangaroos and most wallabies are built for hopping on two legs and not for walking or running. They stand upright, using their long tails as a third foot and their long, powerful hind legs as springboards. The scientific name for kangaroos is *Macropus*, meaning great foot – they have extremely long feet. When hopping, they use their tails for balance and as rudders to help them turn in the air.

Kangaroos graze rather like sheep, moving about slowly in search of grass to eat and water to drink. They move a metre at a time from place to place. But when they are frightened or being chased, they can make great leaps and travel fast and far.

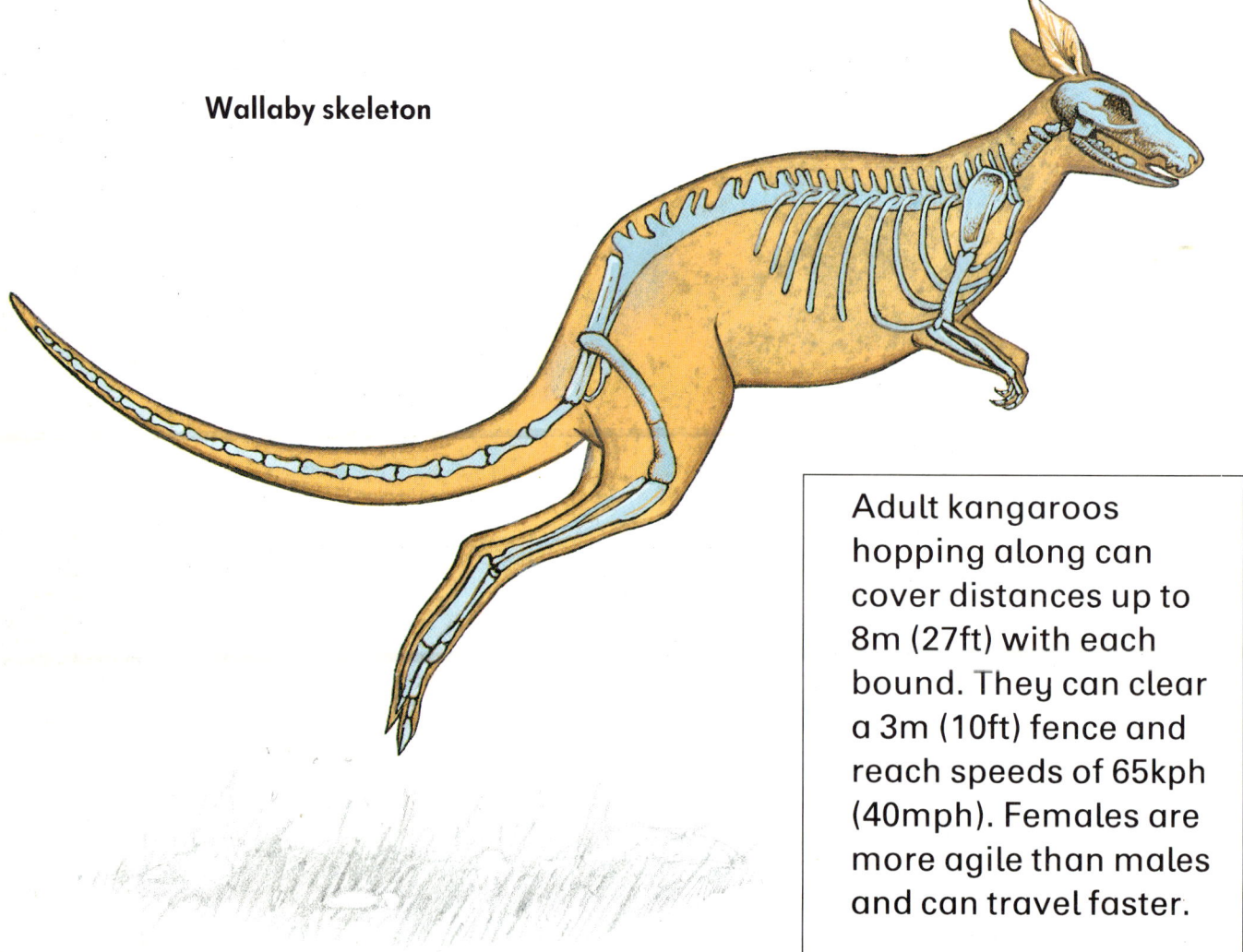

Wallaby skeleton

Adult kangaroos hopping along can cover distances up to 8m (27ft) with each bound. They can clear a 3m (10ft) fence and reach speeds of 65kph (40mph). Females are more agile than males and can travel faster.

A wallaby hops along ▷

Glider

Climbers, gliders and burrowers

Tree kangaroos and the Koala live in forests. They are built for climbing, not hopping. Their front and back pairs of legs are almost the same length. With their back legs, these marsupials can cling to and push themselves up tree trunks. They move among the trees, grasping the branches with their strong hands.

Gliders are pouched mammals that live in woodlands and forests. They have flaps of furred skin stretched between their front and back legs. With the flaps outstretched, the animals can glide 100m (330ft) between tree tops. But gliders do not land gently. They bump into trees at quite high speeds. They use their long claws to fasten onto the trees.

Marsupial Mole

Other marsupials are burrowers. The marsupial mole burrows underground to feed on insect larvae. It has stubby limbs and claws for scraping and pushing away soil.

◁ **A Koala climbing in a eucalyptus tree**

A Virginia Opossum clings to a branch with its claws ▷

Plant-eaters

The Koala, which grows to 60cm (24in) tall and 10kg (22lb) in weight, is a very fussy eater. It will only eat the leaves of eucalyptus trees. It feeds from dusk onwards, and in a single night it eats up to 1kg (2lb) of leaves. It sometimes stores food in its cheek pouches and dozes off to sleep during a meal.

Wombats have gnawing teeth like a squirrel's. They live in burrows by day and come out at night to feed on grasses, bark and fungi. Some possums and gliders make notches in the bark of trees with their teeth and lick up the sweet, sugary gum. Others feed on the pollen and nectar of forest flowers. Marsupials such as the Spotted Cuscus of New Guinea eat insects, birds and their eggs, as well as plants.

Yellow-bellied Glider eating tree gum

Honey Possum eating nectar

Koala eating eucalyptus leaves

The Honey Possum is a mouse-sized marsupial of south-west Australia. It eats nectar and pollen using its brush-tipped tongue to probe deep into flowers.

A Tasmanian Devil showing jaws and teeth ▷

Meat-eaters

Many different types of pouched mammal feed on the flesh of other animals. They include the 80 species of American opossums, the bandicoots and Numbat of Australia, and the Tasmanian Devil.

Marsupial carnivores are often called cats. This is because, like true cats, they are hunters and have pointed canine teeth and sharp claws. But the Pilbara Ningaui is a marsupial which is mouse-like in both size and looks and it feeds on insects. The Spotted-tailed Quoll looks like a weasel and it feeds on small wallabies. The Tasmanian Devil, which grows to 90cm (35in) from head to tail, often hunts lambs and chickens, but prefers to scavenge on dead animals.

The Pilbara Ningaui eats insects

An antechinus eats small lizards

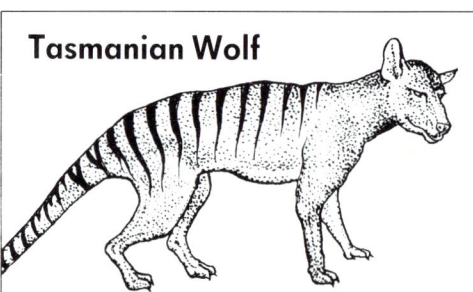

Tasmanian Wolf

The Tasmanian Wolf was a dog-like pouched mammal that was found all over Tasmania about 100 years ago. It has since been hunted to extinction. It was about 60cm (24in) high and about 80cm (32in) long.

Wombats live in underground homes 50cm (20in) wide and 30m (100ft) long. They feed at night. In winter the Common Wombat, which lives in heaths and on hills, comes out during the day to warm up in the sun.

Wombat burrowing

Daily life

Most marsupials feed at night and rest during the day. The Koala, for example, spends the daytime sleeping, wedged between branches of a eucalyptus tree. At sunset, it climbs to the tree top to feed. Cuscuses, possums and opossums move through forests at night, travelling between feeding and resting sites.

In hot weather, kangaroos feed at dawn and again late at night. They spend the daytime sleeping and sheltering from the sun under trees. In cooler weather, they feed during the day and sleep at night. The Colocolo, a small South American marsupial, lives in cool, damp forests. In winter it hibernates in nests in hollow trees or under tree roots.

A possum feeding in a tree at night ▷

Social life

Kangaroos live in groups called mobs. A mob usually consists of an adult male and two or three females and their young. The young are known as joeys. A baby joey will stay with its mother until it is about 20 months old. Then, every week or two, it may move from one mob to another. When food is easy to find, mobs collect together in groups of 50 or more.

The Koala and most other marsupials live alone. They only seek the company of others at mating time. A male Koala may attract two or three females and mate with each of them. A mother Koala looks after her young until it is about a year old. She carries the youngster on her back as she moves through the trees.

A mob of Red Kangaroos feeding

A young kangaroo looks and listens for its mother ▷

Enemies and defence

Kangaroos have several deadly enemies. The fiercest is the Dingo, the native Australian dog. Only a fully grown kangaroo can match the Dingo's fighting skills. When cornered, a kangaroo will kick with its hind legs and use its claws to rip at its enemy's flesh. Joey kangaroos are often preyed on by eagles and foxes. The Koala is also killed by Dingos and by large lizards.

Many of the small marsupials, such as bandicoots, can scurry away quickly when danger threatens. Most of them go unnoticed, however, because their fur is coloured to blend in with their background. Opossums act dead, or "play possum" when in danger. As most hunting animals prefer to kill their victims, they leave the opossums alone.

Dingos are the size of a collie. They are placental mammals. They hunt alone, in pairs, or in small packs. They prey on all kinds of marsupial. They creep up on their victims and then pounce. They live in the forests and open grasslands of central Australia.

The Dingo

Eastern Barred Bandicoot

◁ **A kangaroo escapes from a pack of dingos**

The big eyes of this cuscus help it to see well at night ▷

At mating time, a male Koala attracts females and warns off other males with growling calls that sound like a chain-saw. A female Koala that is not ready to mate uses a wailing distress call to discourage males.

A male and female Sugar Glider rub each other with their body scents so that they will be able to recognise one another

Senses and scents

A marsupial's most important senses are hearing and smell. Kangaroos have long ear flaps which they can turn backwards and forwards to hear sounds from all directions. Antechinuses and other meat-eaters that hunt at night use hearing to locate and home in on their prey. Most tree-dwellers use sounds to keep in touch with one another at a distance.

Possums and gliders live in a world of smells and body scents. They mark their areas with their urine and dung, and rub one another with scents from their skin glands. Brushtail possums and cuscuses rely more on vision than hearing for their survival in the forests. They have large, forward facing eyes that help them judge distances accurately.

Courtship and breeding

Female kangaroos are ready to mate and have babies when they are about 18 months old. Male kangaroos are about 3½ years old before they can mate. Generally, kangaroos mate in summer so that the joeys are ready to leave the pouch the following spring.

Male kangaroos often fight with one another for the right to mate with a female. The winner then courts the female by nuzzling her and wooing her with clucking noises. The pair then mate. The female produces just one baby at a time. As soon as the baby is born, it makes its way to its mother's pouch and searches for one of her four teats to get milk. The mother is then ready to mate again.

Female Virginia Opossums produce up to 50 young at a time. But most of these die as they never find their way to one of their mother's 13 tiny teats.

Reproduction of the Red Kangaroo

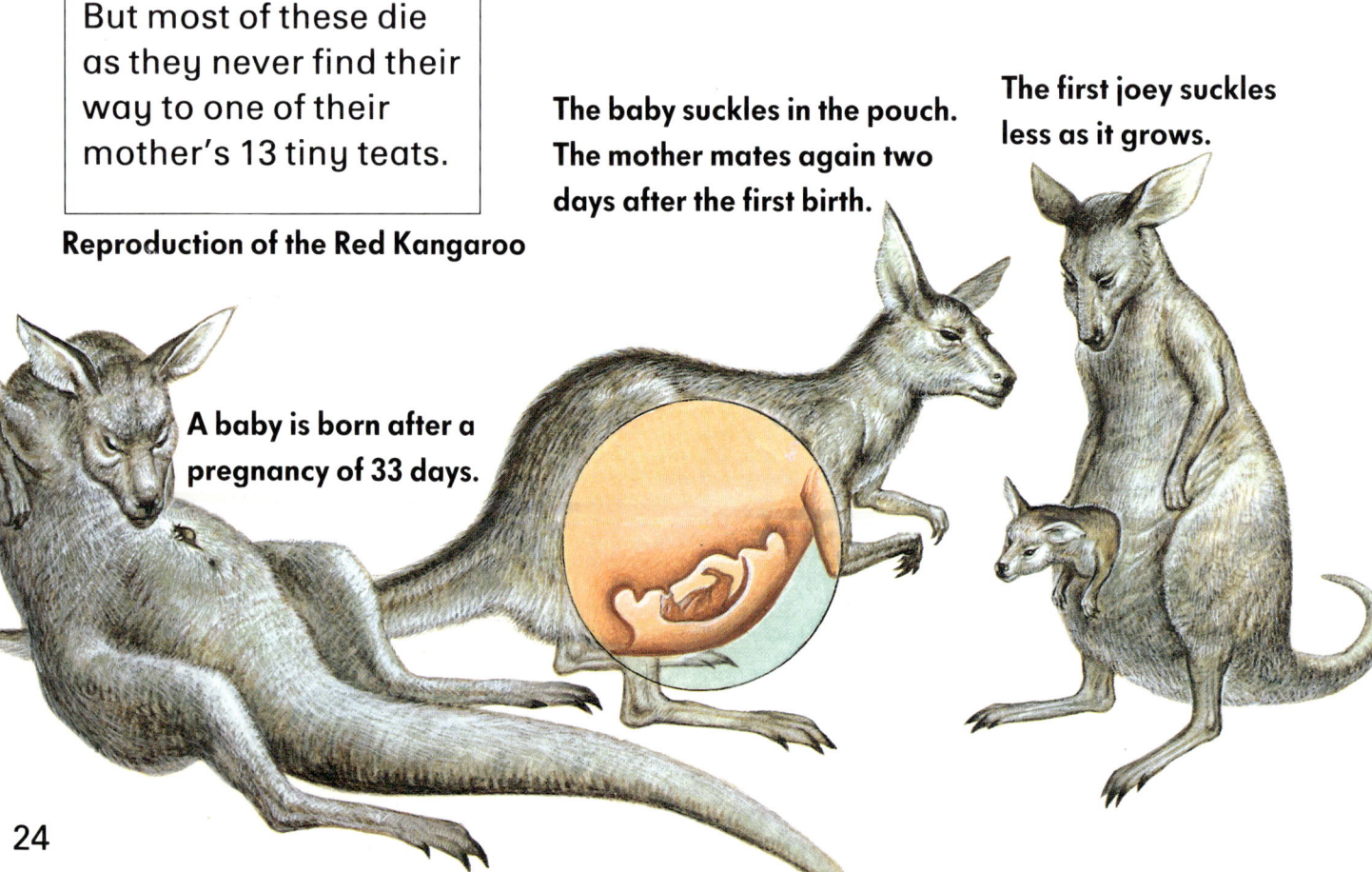

A baby is born after a pregnancy of 33 days.

The baby suckles in the pouch. The mother mates again two days after the first birth.

The first joey suckles less as it grows.

A mother Koala and her infant rest in a tree during the day

A second baby is born after the first joey has left the pouch (seven months after it was born).

The first joey now eats plant food, but still suckles. The second joey suckles constantly.

Growing up

A newborn kangaroo has no ears, no eyes and no fur. It looks more like a baby mouse than a kangaroo. Using the claws on its tiny front limbs, it climbs into its mother's pouch. This 15cm (6in) journey takes about three minutes. Here it gets food, warmth and protection. When it is about five months old, the joey pokes its head out of the pouch for the first time. Over the next few months, it leaves the pouch for longer periods each day. It starts to hop, to feed on grass and to clean itself. But whenever it is frightened, it pops back into its mother's pouch.

Joeys are very playful. They wrestle and box with one another. This is good practice for defending themselves against dingos and foxes. It is also practice for male kangaroos which fight to win females when they are adult. Kangaroos live for up to 18 years in the wild and 28 years in captivity.

A newborn kangaroo must find its way to one of its mother's teats and quickly start to take milk, otherwise it dies. It gets no help from its mother. As it suckles, the teat swells and fills its mouth. This means the mother cannot dislodge her young when she moves around. The baby grows quickly but it is a month or more before it starts to look like its parents.

Young Red Kangaroos fighting

The two opponents approach one another, stalking about and scratching as if preparing for battle.

Opossum babies on their mother's back

They lock their forearms together and wrestle.

Then they try and push each other to the ground.

Survival file

In Australia, marsupials have suffered greatly since the arrival of European people in the 1770s. Before then the native Aborigines hunted most species of marsupial for meat, but they never killed large numbers of the animals. The Europeans brought with them sheep, cattle, rabbits, foxes, cats and dogs, and they cleared forests to graze their animals. The kangaroos ate much of the grass that the farmers needed for their sheep and cattle, so they were regarded as pests and shot in their thousands.

An abandoned joey is rescued after its mother has been killed

Until the 1930s, the Koala and other marsupials were shot for sport. Others were killed for their fur. As forests were cut down, the homes of tree-living species such as the cuscuses and brushtail possums were destroyed. All marsupials became easy prey to foxes, or to cats and dogs that became wild.

Koalas are removed from the wild to protected areas

Hunting of marsupials is largely forbidden today in Australia. The Koala live mainly in special reserves and there are protected areas of temperate and tropical forests where most species are able to live freely. The large Red, Grey and Hill Kangaroos, however, sometimes roam *too* freely over the open grasslands. Occasionally they have to be shot or poisoned in large numbers to keep their populations at reasonable levels.

In South America, the greatest threat to the opossums was, and still is, the destruction of their forest homes. In North America, however, opossums are not endangered, despite being hunted for food and their fur. Many live on farms and in towns. The Virginia Opossum can now be found as far north as Canada.

Kangaroos are sometimes killed to keep their numbers down

Identification chart

This chart shows you a wide variety of pouched mammals, most of which can be seen in zoos. They range in size from the Red Kangaroo to the Woolly Opossum and the Sugar Glider. Notice how only the kangaroos and wallabies are built for hopping along. Each square represents 30cm (12in).

🟠 Australian species
🟢 American species

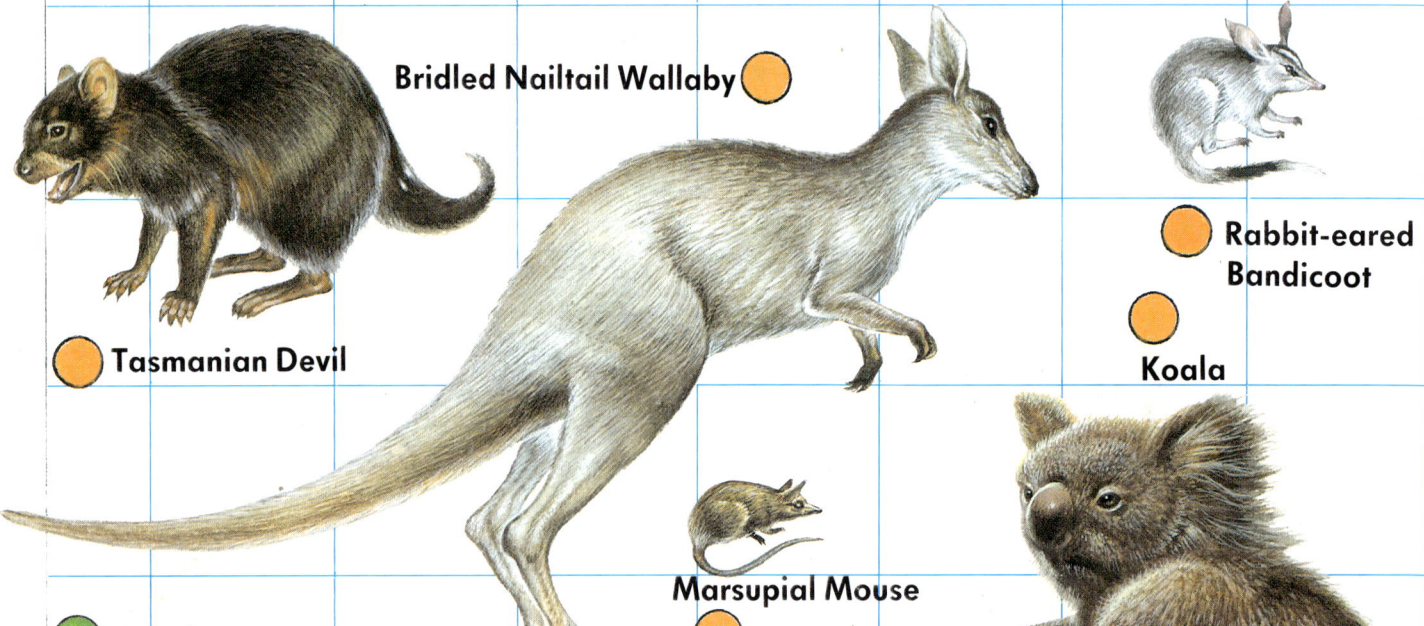

Bridled Nailtail Wallaby
Tasmanian Devil
Rabbit-eared Bandicoot
Koala
Marsupial Mouse
Yapok
Marsupial Mole

Make the Marsupial Game
1. Draw and colour board as shown. Number squares 1 to 100.
2. Make counters using card.
3. Write out question cards using the table provided. Add more of your own animals to the list.
4. To play, take turns to throw the dice and move forwards, starting from 1. Each time you land on a coloured square, take a question card. If you get the correct answer, move on 4 squares. If you get it wrong, go back 4.

1.									
91	92	93	94	95	96	97	98	99	100
90	89	88	87	86	85	84	83	82	81
71	72	73	74	75	76	77	78	79	80
70	69	68	67	66	65	64	63	62	61
51	52	53	54	55	56	57	58	59	60
50	49	48	47	46	45	44	43	42	41
31	32	33	34	35	36	37	38	39	40
30	29	28	27	26	25	24	23	22	21
11	12	13	14	15	16	17	18	19	20
10	9	8	7	6	5	4	3	2	1

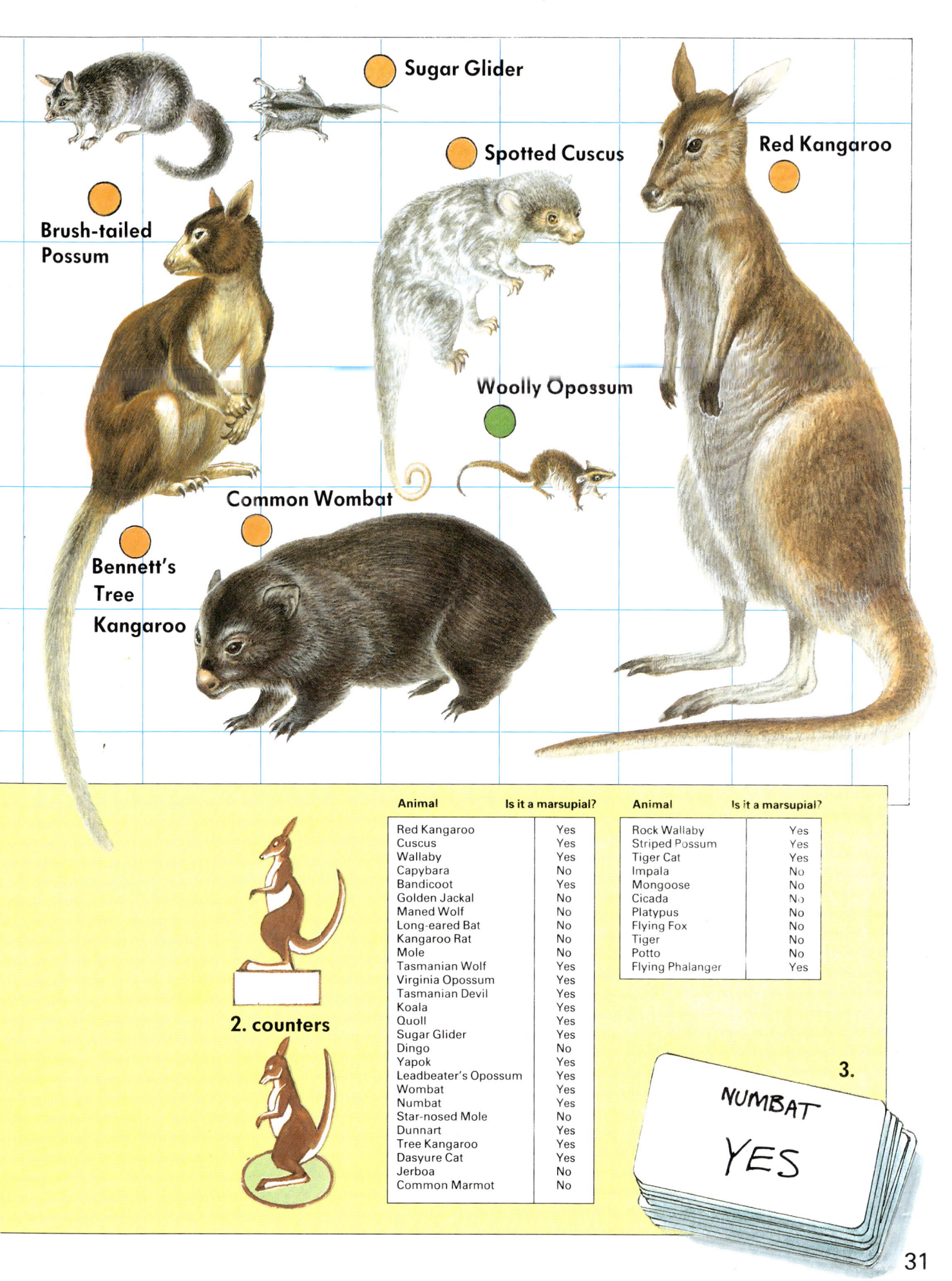

Index

A Antechinus 14, 22

B babies 7, 18, 24, 25
Bandicoots 14, 21
boxing 26-27
breeding 24
Brush-tailed
 Possums 22, 29, 31
burrowing 11, 16

C cheek pouches 12
claws 11, 12, 14, 21, 26
climbing 11
Colocolo 16
courtship 24
Cuscuses 16, 22, 27

E ears 22
enemies 21
eyes 22

F feeding and food 5, 7, 8, 11, 12, 14, 16, 26
feet 8

G Gliders 11, 12, 22, 30, 31
Grey Kangaroo 7, 29

H hands 11
Hill Kangaroo 29
Honey Possum 12
hopping 8, 26

J joeys (young) 18, 21, 24, 25, 26, 28

K Kangaroos – see Red, Grey, Tree kangaroos, land Wallabies.
Koalas 5, 11, 12, 16, 18, 21, 22, 24, 29, 30

L *legs 8, 11, 21
limbs 11, 26

M Marsupial mole 11, 30
Marsupial mouse 7, 30
mating 18, 22, 24
mobs 18

N Numbat 14

O Opossums 5, 14, 16, 21, 24, 27, 29

P Pilbara Ningaui 14
Possums 3, 5, 12, 16, 22
pouch 5, 7, 24, 26

Q Quoll, Spotted-tailed 14

R Red Kangaroo 5, 7, 18, 24, 26, 29, 30, 31

S scent 22
senses 22

T tail 8
Tasmanian Devil 14, 30
Tasmanian Wolf 14
teeth 12, 13, 14
tongue 12
Tree kangaroos 11, 31

W Wallabies 5, 8, 30
Wombats 5, 12, 16

Y Yapok 30

Photographic Credits: Cover and pages 6, 10, 13, 15, 18, 25, 27, 28 and 29 (left): Bruce Coleman; title page and pages 4, 17, 19 and 29 (right): Planet Earth: page 9: NHPA; page 20 (all): Ardea.